THE SNOWS
OF KILIMANJARO

Dan Leathers

Mitchell Lane
PUBLISHERS

P.O. Box 196
Hockessin, Delaware 19707
Visit us on the web: www.mitchelllane.com
Comments? email us: mitchelllane@mitchelllane.com

Mitchell Lane
PUBLISHERS

Printing   1   2   3   4   5   6   7   8   9

A Robbie Reader/On the Verge of Extinction: Crisis in the Environment

Library of Congress Cataloging-in-Publication Data
Leathers, Dan.
   The snows of Kilimanjaro / by Dan Leathers.
      p. cm. — (A Robbie reader. On the verge of extinction)
   Includes bibliographical references and index.
   Audience: K to grade 3.
   ISBN-13: 978-1-58415-584-3 (lib. bdg.)
1. Nature—Effect of human beings on—Tanzania—Kilimanjaro, Mount-—Juvenile literature.
2. Glaciers—Tanzania—Kilimanjaro, Mount—Juvenile literature. 3. Global warming—Tanzania—Kilimanjaro, Mount—Juvenile literature. 4. Kilimanjaro, Mount (Tanzania)—Environmental conditions—Juvenile literature. I. Title.
   GF729.L43 2008
   551.31'20967826—dc22

                                                                                          2007000815

ABOUT THE AUTHOR: Dr. Daniel Leathers has been fascinated with the earth's environment since childhood. This fascination has developed into a career, teaching about and researching our amazing planet. He attended Lycoming College and the Pennsylvania State University, earning degrees in physics, meteorology, and geography. He currently teaches in the Geography Department at the University of Delaware. He is the author of more than 35 scientific articles and numerous popular publications. He lives in the Amish country of Pennsylvania with his wife and two daughters.

PHOTO CREDITS: pp. 7, 10, 11, 20, 26—Jupiterimages Corporation; pp. 4, 18—Jonathan Scott; pp. 8, 12—NASA; pp. 14, 16, 17, 19, 22, 24, 25—Barbara Marvis; p. 20—Africa Environment Outlook; p. 25—Peccadilles

TABLE OF CONTENTS

Words in **bold** type can be found in the glossary.

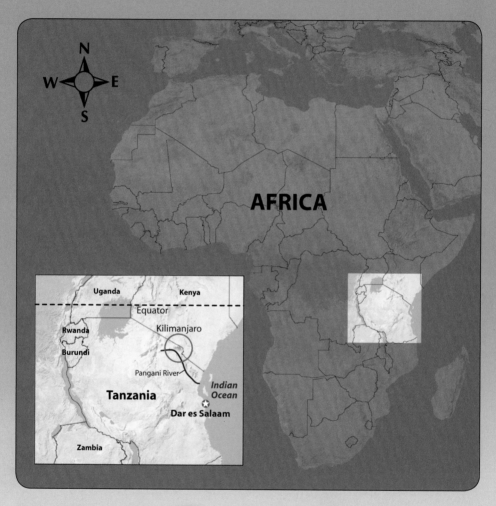

Mount Kilimanjaro is located in Tanzania on the continent of Africa. It lies just below the equator, where the weather is very warm all year round.

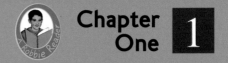

THE SHINING MOUNTAIN

German missionary Johannes Rebmann followed his African guides over flat, dry land. He was exploring the eastern part of Africa, near the Indian Ocean. Rebmann's guides had told him about a "shining mountain" and the Jagga (or Chaga) people who lived there.

After two weeks, in November 1848, they spotted it. Rebmann wrote in his diary: "This morning we discerned [saw] the Mountains of Jagga more distinctly than ever; and about ten o'clock I fancied I saw a dazzlingly white cloud. My guide called the white which I saw merely 'Beredi,' cold; it was perfectly clear to me, however, that it could be nothing else but 'snow.' "

The next year, when Rebmann reported what he had seen in Africa, scientists in Europe didn't believe him. Most people thought that he was lying or crazy. Rebmann said the mountain was very near the earth's **equator** (ee-KWAY-tur). The equator is the imaginary line that circles the earth halfway between the North Pole and the South Pole. Temperatures near the equator are usually very warm. How could the mountain be covered with snow?

As more and more people from Europe explored this part of Africa, Rebmann was proved correct. The shining mountain, called Kilimanjaro (kih-lih-man-JAR-oh), was definitely covered in snow.

Mount Kilimanjaro has become known as one of the most beautiful places in the world. It is a popular place with **tourists** (TOOR-ist). Between 15,000 and 25,000 people climb Mount Kilimanjaro each year. Many other people just come to look at it. Lately,

When Johannes Rebmann first saw Mount Kilimanjaro, the top was covered in snow. It looked like a shiny white cloud.

people have noticed that there seems to be less and less snow and ice on the mountain. If all the snow and ice disappears, the lives of many people will be changed forever.

Uhuru Peak on Kibo Summit is the highest point on Mount Kilimanjaro. At one time, it was surrounded by snow and glaciers.

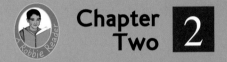

WHY IS THERE SNOW ON KILIMANJARO?

Mount Kilimanjaro is located about 200 miles south of the equator in a country called Tanzania (tan-zah-NEE-uh). It is the tallest mountain in Africa, rising to a height of 19,340 feet (nearly four miles). It is really made up of three separate **volcanoes**: Kibo (19,340 feet), Mawenzi (16,896 feet), and Shira (13,000 feet). All three volcanoes are **dormant** (DOR-munt), which means that they do not erupt much anymore, but they still could someday.

The mountain is surrounded by flat land covered with tall grasses, shrubs, and a few trees. The Serengeti (sayr-en-GEH-tee) Plains, which are famous for their beauty

Elephants roam the Serengeti Plains near Mount Kilimanjaro. The Serengeti is the world's largest animal refuge.

and their many animals, are not far from Kilimanjaro.

Places that are this close to the equator are usually very warm, because the sun is high in the sky every day during the year. The sun heats up the land, making the air warmer, too. The land around Mount Kilimanjaro is very warm and dry most of the year. So why is there snow on Mount Kilimanjaro?

For snow to fall, temperatures must be below freezing, and there must be water

vapor (VAY-pur) in the air. The air at the top of Mount Kilimanjaro is much colder than the air at the bottom of the mountain. Normal temperatures at the bottom are about 86 degrees **Fahrenheit** (FAA-ren-hyt), like a hot summer day. At the top, they are only 15 degrees Fahrenheit or lower. Since water freezes at 32 degrees Fahrenheit, temperatures near the top of the mountain are below freezing almost all the time. It is cold enough to snow. But where does the water come from?

Clouds over Mount Kilimanjaro hold water vapor. At the cold mountaintop, the vapor will fall as snow.

1912

Kilimanjaro,
Africa

1970

2000

Photographs of the mountain since 1912 show how the
snows have been disappearing at an alarming rate.

Mount Kilimanjaro is close to the Indian Ocean on the east side of Africa. Air that blows in from the ocean has a lot of water in it. As the air reaches a mountain like Kilimanjaro, it has to rise up and over the mountain. As the air rises over Kilimanjaro, it cools down, and it can't hold as much water. Most of the water in the air comes out as rain. This keeps the lower parts of Mount Kilimanjaro very wet. As the air goes farther up the mountain, the air becomes drier. What little water remains in the air falls as snow near the cold top of the mountain.

If the temperature near the top of the mountain warms up, there may be less snow. Also, if the amount of water vapor in the air decreases, there may be less snow. Are either of these things causing the snows of Kilimanjaro to disappear?

The glaciers on Kilimanjaro are getting smaller. They are not as wide or as thick as they were when Johannes Rebmann first explored the mountain. Scientists are trying to find out why.

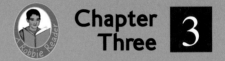
WHY ARE THE SNOWS DISAPPEARING?

For many years, scientists have been trying to understand why the snow and ice on Kilimanjaro have been disappearing. There are several possible reasons, but first it is important to understand exactly what is disappearing.

Year after year, as the snow piles up on the mountaintop, it changes and becomes **glacier** (GLAY-shur) ice, like a huge ice cube. Scientists believe that the glaciers on Mount Kilimanjaro have been there for at least 10,000 years. Since the late 1900s, the glaciers have been shrinking faster and faster. Some scientists believe they will be completely gone by 2015 if they keep

Hikers near the top of the mountain have to dress for the extreme cold. Although temperatures there may be rising, they are not hot enough to melt the glaciers.

shrinking this fast. But what is making them shrink?

There are several different ways to get rid of ice. When an ice cube sits in a warm room, it slowly melts into a puddle of water. At first, many scientists thought the glaciers on Mount Kilimanjaro were melting, too. They thought that the glaciers were melting due to **global warming** (GLOH-bul WAR-ming). Global warming is a rise in the temperature of the whole earth. Many scientists believe global warming is caused by certain gases that humans have put into the air. These gases come from things like cars and factories.

However, the more that scientists have studied the snows on Kilimanjaro, the more they believe something else is happening. They say the temperatures on the mountain are not high enough for the glaciers to melt. Instead, they have come up with another **theory** (THEER-ee) for how the glaciers are disappearing.

Glacier ice melts faster at the edges, near bare ground.

If you leave an ice cube in your freezer for a very long time, it will slowly shrink. It shrinks even though it doesn't melt. It changes directly from a solid (ice) to a gas (water vapor in the air). This type of change is called **sublimation** (sub-lih-MAY-shun).

Sublimation is a lot like **evaporation** (ee-vah-puh-RAY-shun). Every time liquid water slowly disappears, it is changing to gas (water vapor in the air). It is evaporating.

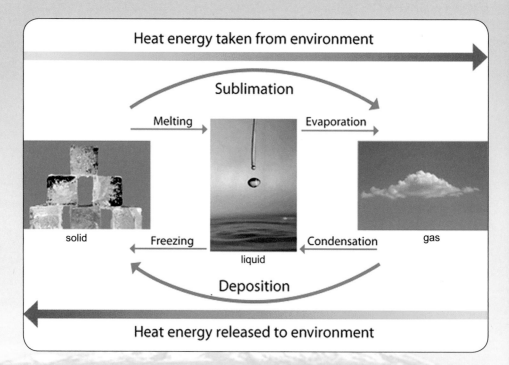

Water can take the form of solid ice, liquid water, or vapor (gas). When it changes from liquid to vapor, it evaporates. When it changes directly from ice to vapor, the process is called sublimation.

Six out of every ten people who hike up Mount Kilimanjaro will reach the top. The rest will turn back. Although the climb is not very steep, the air near the top is very thin. The lack of air can make people sick.

Scientists have learned that the air near the top of Kilimanjaro has been getting drier. The air is drier because the weather of eastern Africa is different than it was when Johannes Rebmann first visited the area. It is also drier because of changes humans are making to the environment. As a result, there has been less snow falling on the mountain. With less snow, no new glacier ice has been able to form.

A woman harvests coffee beans near Mount Kilimanjaro. Organizations such as the African Blackwood Conservation Project have been working to replace the trees that were cut down for coffee plants.

Scientists believe that humans have also caused more sublimation to happen on Kilimanjaro. Since about 1900, people have cut down the thick forests that covered the lower parts of the mountain. Now these areas are covered with plants that people grow to sell, such as coffee. When the forest covered the mountain, the winds rising up the mountain were very moist. Sublimation happens more slowly in moist air than in dry air. When the forests were cut down, the air rising up the mountain was much drier. This drier air has made sublimation of the glaciers happen faster.

With the drier air, less snow falls on the mountain. Sublimation speeds up. The glaciers shrink very fast.

Most scientists now believe that drier weather and changes made on the mountain by humans have caused the glaciers to shrink. Unless more snow begins to fall on the mountaintop soon, it is likely that the glaciers will disappear completely. There will no longer be snows on Kilimanjaro.

It takes about four or five days to hike to the top of Kilimanjaro. The hardest parts of the climb are crossing the slopes of loose rocks called scree, and then crossing the slippery glaciers.

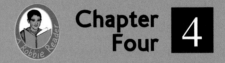

DO THE GLACIERS REALLY MATTER?

If the glaciers of Kilimanjaro disappear completely, it will cause many problems for the people of Tanzania and the rest of east Africa. Nearly one million people live in the area around Mount Kilimanjaro. Many of these people make their money from tourists. If the glaciers disappear, it is likely that fewer tourists will visit the area. People who make their money from tourists will find it harder to make a living.

Water that runs down the mountain flows into the Pangani (pahn-GAH-nee) River. This river supplies water for farmers and other people living along its 250-mile length. If less water flows into the Pangani

As the snow and ice continue to disappear, less and less water becomes available for the plants and animals at the bottom of the mountain.

River from Mount Kilimanjaro, the people there will not have enough clean drinking water. Farmers may not have enough water to grow their crops. Animals and fish that live along and in the river will find it harder to survive.

The water in the river is also used to **generate** (JEH-nuh-rayt) electricity for people all across east Africa. If there is not enough water to produce electricity, other sources of power will need to be found. This could be very expensive.

The many people who live along the Pangani River depend on the snows of Mount Kilimanjaro for their survival.

Climbers celebrate reaching Uhuru Peak. If the snows should melt completely, will the tourists stop coming to Tanzania?

The glaciers on Mount Kilimanjaro are not the only mountain glaciers that are shrinking. Many glaciers across the world have been getting smaller. Glaciers grow when the weather is cold and wet. They shrink when it is warmer and dry. Most scientists believe that weather changes, human activity, and global warming are causing glaciers to shrink in many areas.

North America, South America, Europe, Asia, and Antarctica have many glaciers, but Africa has very few. Johannes Rebmann, 160 years ago, saw one of the most stunning sites in the world. He saw the "shining mountain" of the Jagga people. If the glaciers of Africa disappear, one of the most beautiful sights in the world, the snows of Kilimanjaro, will be gone.

Learn More About Africa

Africa is an amazing continent that is unlike any other. Some of the books and web sites listed on page 30 will help you learn more about the land and the people of Africa. Visit your local library and read as many books as you can about the continent. Tell your friends and your teachers what you have learned, and plan a day to celebrate Africa at your school.

Conserve Energy

Many scientists believe that a lot of the earth's mountain glaciers are shrinking because of global warming. The gas that causes this warming is called carbon dioxide. This gas comes from burning things like oil and natural gas to heat our homes, and from gasoline to fuel our cars. You can do simple things to conserve, or save, energy. You can turn the heat down in your house, turn off the light when you leave a room, and walk instead of ride in a car.

Plant Trees

The loss of forests on Mount Kilimanjaro is one reason that the glaciers are disappearing. Trees take carbon dioxide out of the air and give water vapor and oxygen back. Trees also provide homes for all kinds of animals. Ask your parents and teachers to help you plant some trees in your neighborhood or at your school.

Don't Waste Water

Many people in Africa die each year because they don't have enough clean water to drink. Never waste water. For example, turn off the water while you brush your teeth. When water goes down the drain without being used, it has been wasted. You could also convince your family and friends to help you clean up a stream in your area.

Books

Davis, Kenneth C. *Don't Know Much About Planet Earth*. New York: HarperCollins Children's Books, 2001.

Gaff, Jackie. *I Wonder Why Mountains Have Snow on Top: and Other Questions About Mountains*. London: Kingfisher, 2004.

Gallant, Roy A. *Glaciers*. London: Franklin Watts, 1999.

McQuail, Lisa. *The Masai of Africa*. Minneapolis: Lerner Publications, 2002.

Newman, Gwill. *Bingo Bear Was Here: A Toy Bear's Climb to the Top of Africa's Highest Mountain*. Sante Fe, New Mexico: Sunstone Press, 2003.

Sayre, April P. *Africa*. Brookfield, Connecticut: Millbrook Press Inc., 1999.

Simon, Seymour. *Icebergs and Glaciers*. New York: HarperTrophy, 1999.

Taylor, Barbara. *The Earth*. New York: Kingfisher, 2001.

Works Consulted

African Blackwood Conservation Project
http://www.blackwoodconservation.org/kilimanjaro_conservation.html

Climbing Kilimanjaro http://www.climbingkilimanjaro.com/overview.htm

Earth Science Picture of the Day: Mount Kilimanjaro http://epod.usra.edu/archive/epodviewer.php3?oid=120832

Journeys International: Kilimanjaro Facts
http://www.journeys-intl.com/portal/kilimanjaro/kili_facts.html

National Geographic: Mount Kilimanjaro's Glacier Is Crumbling
http://news.nationalgeographic.com/news/2003/09/0923_030923_kilimanjaroglaciers.html

University of North Dakota, Oregon State University: VolcanoWorld
http://volcano.und.edu/vwdocs/volc_images/img_kilimanjaro.html

dormant (DOR-munt)—sleeping, not active.

equator (ee-KWAY-tur)—the imaginary line that circles the earth halfway between the North Pole and the South Pole.

evaporation (ee-vah-puh-RAY-shun)—the process of water changing from a liquid to a vapor (gas).

Fahrenheit (FAA-ren-hyt)—a temperature scale marked in degrees, with water freezing at 32 degrees and boiling at 212 degrees.

generate (JEH-nuh-rayt)—to make or produce.

glacier (GLAY-shur)—a large piece of ice moving very slowly down a slope.

global warming (GLOH-bul WAR-ming)—an overall rise in the earth's temperature associated with increasing amounts of carbon dioxide in the atmosphere.

sublimation (sub-lih-MAY-shun)—the process of water changing from a solid (ice) to a vapor (gas).

theory (THEER-ee)—a belief based on the study of a number of facts.

tourist (TOOR-ist)—a person who is traveling for pleasure.

vapor (VAY-pur)—the gas form of a substance such as water.

volcano (vul-KAY-noh)—a hole in the earth's crust through which lava, steam, gases, and ashes escape.

INDEX